First World War
and Army of Occupation
War Diary
France, Belgium and Germany

39 DIVISION
118 Infantry Brigade
Black Watch (Royal Highlanders)
4th Battalion
1 November 1915 - 15 March 1916

WO95/2591/1

The Naval & Military Press Ltd
www.nmarchive.com
Published in association with The National Archives

Published by

The Naval & Military Press Ltd

Unit 10 Ridgewood Industrial Park,

Uckfield, East Sussex,

TN22 5QE England

Tel: +44 (0) 1825 749494

www.naval-military-press.com

www.nmarchive.com

This diary has been reprinted in facsimile from the original. Any imperfections are inevitably reproduced and the quality may fall short of modern type and cartographic standards.

© **Crown Copyright**
Images reproduced by permission of The National Archives, London, England, 2015.

Contents

Document type	Place/Title	Date From	Date To
Heading	WO95/2591/1 4 Bn Black Watch (Royal Highlanders) Nov 1915-Mar 1916. 39 Div-118 Inf Bde.		
Heading	46th Division 139th Infy Bde. 39 Division 118 Bde 4th Bn Black Watch (Roy. Hdrs) Nov 1915. From 7 (Meerut) Div Bareilley Bde.		
Miscellaneous	Duplicate Copy.		
War Diary		01/11/1915	28/11/1915
Miscellaneous	138		
Miscellaneous	1/4th Bn The Black Watch, T.F.		
Miscellaneous	1/1st Bn The Black Watch T.F.		
Heading	39 Division 118 Bde 4 Bn Black Watch (Royal Highlanders) 1915 Nov-1916 Mar From 7 Meerut Div, Bareilly Bde Amalgamated With 5 Bn Known As 4/5 Bn With 39 Div 118 Bde.		
Heading	139th Inf. Bde. 46th Div. Battn. Transferred From Bareilly Bde. Meerut Div. 6.11.15. Battn. Transferred To 44th Inf. Bde. 15th Div. 15.11.15. 4th Battn. The Black Watch (Royal Highlanders). November 1915		
Heading	War Diary Of 1st/4th Battn. The Black Watch (R.H.) T.F. From November 1st, 1915. To November 30th 1915. (Volume5) III.		
War Diary		01/11/1915	06/11/1915
War Diary		05/11/1915	28/11/1915
Miscellaneous	Appendices.		
Miscellaneous	Appendix 1	04/11/1915	04/11/1915
Miscellaneous	1/4th Bn The Black Watch, T.F.		
Heading	15th Division 44th Infy Bde 39 Division 118 Bde. 1-4th Bn Roy. Hdrs (Blk Watch)-Dec 1915		
Miscellaneous	1/4th Black Watch. December 1915		
Heading	War Diary Of 1st/4th Battn. The Black Watch (R.H) T.F. From 1st December 1915 To 31st December 1915 (Volume 6) IV.		
War Diary		01/12/1915	31/12/1915
Miscellaneous	1/4th Bn. The Black Watch, T.F.		
Heading	51st Division 154th Infy Bde 39 Div 118 Bde 1-4th Bn Black Watch (Roy. Highlanders) Jan-Feb 1916		
Heading	War Diary Of 1st/4th Battn The Black Watch (R.H) T.F. From 1st January 1916 To 31st January 1916 (Volume V).		
War Diary	Allouagne.	01/01/1916	31/01/1916
Miscellaneous	1/4th Bn. The Black Watch (R.H.) T.F.		
Miscellaneous	1/4th Bn. The Black Watch (R.H.) T.F. State For 1st January 1916	01/01/1916	01/01/1916
Heading	War Diary Of 1st/4th Battn. The Black Watch (R.H.) T.F. From 1st February 1916 To 29th February 1916 (Volume VI).		
War Diary	Rainneville Somme.	01/02/1916	29/02/1916
Miscellaneous	Special Order By Brigadier General C.E. Stewart, C.M.G., Commanding 154th Infantry Bde. Appendix No. 1	24/02/1916	24/02/1916

Miscellaneous	1/4th Bn. The Black Watch (R.H.) T.F. State For 1st February 1916	01/02/1916	01/02/1916
Miscellaneous	1/4th Bn. The Black Watch (R.H.) T.F. Casualty List For The Month Of February 1916		
Miscellaneous			
Miscellaneous	1/4th Bn The Black Watch (R.H.) T.F. Officer Reinforcements In February 1916		
War Diary	In The Field.	01/02/1916	01/02/1916
Heading	39 Div 118 Bde 1/4 Black Watch 1916 March (1st To 15).		
Heading	War Diary Of 1/4th Bn The Black Watch War Diary For March 1916 From 1-3-16 To 15-3-16 (Volume Officer Volume For February, 1916). Vol.VII.		
War Diary	Renescure.	01/03/1916	06/03/1916
War Diary	H.A Belle Hotesse.	07/03/1916	15/03/1916
Miscellaneous	O.C. 1/4th Black Watch. Appendix 1	02/03/1916	02/03/1916
Miscellaneous	War Diary For March, 1916. Appendix 2		
Miscellaneous	1/4th. Battalion The Black Watch. War Diary For March 1916. Appendix 3		
Miscellaneous	1/4th Bn. The Black Watch (R.H.), T.F. State For March 1st, 1916. Appendix 4	01/03/1916	01/03/1916
Miscellaneous	1/4th Bn. The Black Watch (R.H.), T.F. State For March 15th, 1916	15/03/1916	15/03/1916
Miscellaneous	1/4th Bn. The Black Watch (R.H.), T.F. Appendix 6		

WO95/2591 — 1

4 Bn Black Watch (Royal Highlanders)

Nov 1915 – Mar 1916

39 Div — 118 Inf Bde

ATTACHED { 46TH DIVISION
             139TH INFY BDE

39 DIVISION
118 BDE

4TH BN BLACK WATCH (ROY. HDRS)

NOV 1915

FROM 7 (MEERUT) DIV
BAREILLY BDE

DUPLICATE COPY

INTELLIGENCE SUMMARY

1/4th Bn. R. Berkshire Regt.

(Erase heading not required)

Summary of Events and Information

FRANCE

BETHUNE
1.11.15
1.45 p.m.

Nov - Dec 1915

4.	In trenches 2nd IV.B, Rue Du Bois. Lahore Division to left. 59th Rifles and 69 d Punjabis to right.	
	Weather wet. Enemy not aggressive.	
5.	Lieut. P. M. MOON wounded at LANSDOWNE POST.	
6.	Battn. relieved by 7th Sherwoods. Relief carried out by daylight. Slight mist prevailing. No casualties sustained.	
	Transferred to 139th Bde. (General SHIPLEY) of 46th Division (General STUART WORTLEY) of XI Corps (General HAKING).	
	No. 6 Coy. to supporting position No. 5 and H.Q. in RICHEBOURG, S.2.A.37	

T.F. 2nd

131

WAR DIARY
or
INTELLIGENCE SUMMARY.

Army Form C. 2118.

133

Place	Date	Hour	Summary of Events and Information	Remarks and references to Appendices
	Nov (contd)		On departure of Lieut.-Col. A.G. WAUCHOPE, 2nd Black Watch, Lieut. R.C. CUNNINGHAM assumed command. Confirms assumed command of 2nd Lt. W.F. WILKIE assumed command of No 1 Company and Lieut. T. STEVENSON continued to command the other Company. Lieut. J.L. PULLAR continued A/Adjutant. C.Q.M.S. W.F. CRIGHTON to be A/S.M.	
	7		Farewell Order issued by Lt-Col. A.G. WAUCHOPE, D.S.O., Attached as Appendix.	
			Major G.A.M.L. SCEALES, 1st Argyll and Sutherland Highlanders, joins Battalion and assumes Command. Companies named A and B.	
	8-10		In billets at RICHEBOURG	

Date	Hour	Summary of Events and Information
Nov. 10		Battn. returned to RUE DU BOIS trenches, rain poured left intermission
		Trenches very wet and falling in. Enemy inaggressive
		Work principally centred in construction of front line trenches
9-11		12 Officers (named in Appendix) join Battn. Fonts Officers nightly do a night's duty in trenches
14		Battn. relieved by 7th Sherwoods. Marched to billets at RICHEBOURG.
		Attached to 4th (Highland) Infy. Bde. General Wilson) of 1st Scottish Division (General McCracken), 4th Corps (General Sir H. RAWLINSON)
15		Battn. entrains at ZELOBES and proceed to GOSNAY.

WAR DIARY
or
INTELLIGENCE SUMMARY.

(Erase heading not required.)

Army Form C. 2118.

Place	Date	Hour	Summary of Events and Information	Remarks and references to Appendices
	Nov 7		Battn moves to billets in LABUISSIÈRE. Time devoted to reorganizing and equipping.	
	20		Inspection by Major General commanding 15th Division.	
	24		Draft of 15 ringers join.	
	25		Battn moves to GOSNAY. Major J.B. MUIR joins Battn. from home as 2nd in Command.	
	26		Inspection by G.O.C. 44th Bde.	
	28		Formation of C Coy, composed of Machine Gun detachment, Signallers, Trench Mortar detachment, Stretcher Bearers, and all Officers, N.C.Os. and men not doing duty in the ranks of other Companies. Lt. R.C. CUNNINGHAM to Command.	

WAR DIARY
or
INTELLIGENCE SUMMARY

Army Form C. 2118.

136

Appendix 1.

From Battalion Orders, 4th Bn. The Black Watch (R.H.) T.F. Nov. 4. 95.

Farewell Order by Lt. Col. A.G. Wauchope, D.S.O.

On handing over the command of the 4th R. Black Watch to my Successor, I wish to say how greatly indebted I am to my friends of all ranks during the many trying times of the past six weeks. The work done by the non-commd. officers & men was in every way higher than I thought possible. I can never forget that all ranks did their utmost to take nearly every trench the whole of the Hun position & that a marginal section of the Battalion held a most important section of the true mine under heavy fire & in response after the losses at 3rd Ypres. The full retirement that call, and in the sport of the traditions of the Black Watch, performed the kind valour asked of it.

WAR DIARY or INTELLIGENCE SUMMARY

Army Form C. 2118.

1/4th Bn. The Black Watch T.F.

Place	Date	Hour	Summary of Events and Information	Remarks and references to Appendices
			Appendix 1 (Cont'd).	FRANCE.
			It is with great regret that I hear the 4th Black Watch.	BETHUNE
			I wish the Battalion was to come with the 2nd Battalion and	2nd Ed.
			that we could continue fighting side by side as we have done	1-20
			for the past nine months.	
			But I am also glad that their my representation will soon	
			be carried out and that a separate Commanding Officer will be	
			appointed to the 4th, one who, although he cannot have the	
			interests of the 4th more at heart than I have, will be able	
			to devote his whole time to the needs of the Battalion.	
			I hope too that my second representation will be	
			attended to and that the Battalion will be given a long and	
			well deserved rest out of the trenches.	
			On behalf of the 2nd Battalion I wish to thank all	
			ranks 4th Battalion I can wish the Battalion nothing better	
			than they continue to fight in the same gallant way that	

(Signed) A. G. Wauchope, Lt-Col.,
Commanding
2nd and 1/4th T.F. Battalion
The Black Watch

In the Field
4-11-15

1/4th Bn. The Black Watch, T.F.

List of Officers joining as Reinforcements during the month of November, 1915.

Nov. 7	MAJOR	SCEALES, G.A.M.L.	from 1st Gen.Bn.
" 12	LIEUT.	PLIMPTON, R.A.	13 A.R.dd
" "	"	CURREY, R.F.	13 A.R.dd
" "	2/Lt.	MITCHELL, A.	11 Gen.H
" "	"	JAMES, H.	11 Gen.d
" "	"	FINLAYSON, F.W.N.	11 Gen.H
" "	"	HOWARD BUCHANAN, F.H.	11 Gen.
" "	"	MOSER, G.R.	13 A.R.dd
" "	"	SCRATTON, G.H.	13 A.R.dd
" 14	LIEUT.	ROBERTSON, W.S.	11 B.W.
" "	2/Lt.	MENZIES, J.D.S.	11 B.W.
" "	"	ANDREW, T.F.	11 B.W.
" "	"	OSBORNE, E.C.	11 B.W.
" 25	MAJOR	MUIR, J.B.	rejoined from Res. Bn. B.W.

G.M.L. Sceales
Lieut-Colonel,
COMMANDING 1/4th BATT. THE BLACK WATCH (T.F.)

1/4th Bn. The Black Watch T.F.

Casualty List for the Month of November 1915.

Date	Killed	Wounded	Missing	Sick	Accidentally Killed	Accidentally Wounded
Nov 3				4		
5		1		2		
6				1		
8				2		
9				2		
10				5		
11		3				
12				4		
13				3		
14				1		
15				4		
16				1		
19				1		3
22				1		
27		1				
29				2		
30				1		2
	—	5	—	34	—	5

Officers.
Nov. 5. Wounded — 2nd Lieut: P. M. Moon.

G W M Sack
Lieut-Colonel,
COMMANDING 1/4H BATT. THE BLACK WATCH (T.F.)

39 DIVISION
118 BDE

4 BN BLACK WATCH (ROYAL HIGHLANDERS)

1915 NOV - 1916 MAR

FROM 7 MEERUT DIV, BAREILLY BDE

AMALGAMATED WITH 5 BN.
KNOWN AS 4/5 BN
WITH 39 DIV 118 BDE

139th Inf.Bde.
46th Div.

Battn. transferred
from Bareilly Bde.
Meerut Div. 6.11.15.

Battn. transferred
to 44th Inf.Bde.
15th Div. 15.11.15.

4th BATTN. THE BLACK WATCH (ROYAL HIGHLANDERS).

N O V E M B E R

1 9 1 5

Attached:

Appendices.

Army Form C. 2118.

1/4th Bn. The Black Watch, T.F.

WAR DIARY
or
~~INTELLIGENCE SUMMARY.~~
(Erase heading not required.)

Remarks and references to Appendices
XLVI – DIVISION Nov. 5th–14.
Nov. 14–30.

XLVI
in
XV

Confidential.

War Diary
of
1st/4th Battn. The Black Watch (R.H.) T.F.

From November 1st 1915, to November 30th 1915.

(Volume V) III

George M Searle
Lieut-Colonel,
COMMANDING 1/4th BATT. THE BLACK WATCH T.F.

Army Form C. 2118.

WAR DIARY
or
INTELLIGENCE SUMMARY.
(Erase heading not required.)

1/4th Bn. The Black Watch, T.F.

Place	Date	Hour	Summary of Events and Information	Remarks and references to Appendices
	Nov. 1-6		In trenches 2nd IV B, RUE DU BOIS. Lahore Division to left. 58th Rifles and 69th Punjabis to right.	FRANCE BETHUNE 2nd Edn. 1-40,000
			Weather wet. Enemy not aggressive.	
		5.	Lieut. P.M. MOON wounded at LANSDOWNE POST.	
		6.	Battn. relieved by 7th Sherwoods. Relief carried out by daylight. Slight mist prevailing. No casualties occurred.	
			Transferred to 139th Bde. (General SHIPLEY) of 46th Division (General STUART WORTLEY) of XI Corps (General HAKING).	
			No.6 Coy. to supporting posts, No.5 and H.Q. to billets in RICHEBURG, S.2.A.3.7	

Army Form C. 2118.

WAR DIARY
or
INTELLIGENCE SUMMARY.
(Erase heading not required.)

1/4th Bn. The Black Watch T.F.

Place	Date	Hour	Summary of Events and Information	Remarks and references to Appendices
	Nov. (cont.)		On departure of Lieut-Col. A.G. WAUCHOPE, 2nd Black Watch, Lieut. R.C. CUNNINGHAM assumed command. Companies renamed 1 and 2. 2nd Lt. W.F. WILKIE assumed command of No 1 Company and Lieut. T. STEVENSON continued to command the other Company. Lieut J.L. PULLAR continued A/Adjutant, C.Q.M.S. W.F. CRIGHTON to be A/S.M.	FRANCE BETHUNE 2nd Bn 1-40,000
	7		Farewell Order issued by Lt-Col. A.G. WAUCHOPE, D.S.O., Attached as Appendix. Major G.A. McL. SCEALES, 1st Argyll and Sutherland Highlanders, joins Battalion and assumes Command. Companies renamed A and B.	
	8-10		In billets at RICHEBOURG.	

Army Form C. 2118.

WAR DIARY
or
INTELLIGENCE SUMMARY.

(Erase heading not required.)

1/4th Bn. The Black Watch, T.F.

Place	Date	Hour	Summary of Events and Information	Remarks and references to Appendices
	Nov. 10		Battn. returns to RUE DU BOIS trenches, now named Left Sub-section.	FRANCE BETHUNE 2nd Edn. 1-40,000.
			Trenches very wet and falling in. Enemy unaggressive.	
	9-11		Work principally centered in construction of second line breastwork.	
			12 Officers (named in Appendix) join Battn. Four Officers nightly do a night's duty in trenches.	
	14		Battn. relieved by 7th Sherwoods. Marched to billets at RICHEBOURG.	
			Attached to 44th (Highland) Infy Bde (General WILLISON) of 15th Eastrick Division (General McCRACKEN), 4th Corps (General Sir H. RAWLINSON).	
	15		Battn. embus at ZELOBES and proceed to GOSNAY.	

Army Form C. 2118.

WAR DIARY
or
INTELLIGENCE SUMMARY.
(Erase heading not required.)

1/4th Bn. The Black Watch T.F.

Place	Date	Hour	Summary of Events and Information	Remarks and references to Appendices
	Nov. 17		Battn. moves to billets in LABUISSIÈRE. Time devoted to reorganising and equipping	FRANCE BETHUNE 2nd & 3rd 1-49,000
	20.		Inspection by Major General commanding 15th Division.	
	24.		Draft of 15 privates join.	
	25.		Battn. moves to GOSNAY. Major J.B. MUIR joins Battn. from home as 2nd in Command.	
	26		Inspection by G.O.C. 44th Bde.	
	28.		Formation of C Coy. composed of Machine Gun detachment, Signallers, Trench Mortar detachment, Stretcher Bearers, and all Officers, N.C.O.s and men not doing duty in the ranks of their Companies. Lt.-R.C. CUNNINGHAM to command.	

A P P E N D I C E S .

Army Form C. 2118.

1/4th Bn. The Black Watch T.F.

WAR DIARY
or
INTELLIGENCE SUMMARY.
(Erase heading not required.)

Summary of Events and Information

Appendix 1.

From Battalion Orders, 1/4th Bn. The Black Watch (R.H.) T.F., Nov 4, 1915.

Farewell Order by Lt-Col. A.G. Wauchope, D.S.O.

On handing over the command of the 4th Black Watch I wish to say that I very greatly appreciate the loyal co-operation of all Ranks during the very trying time of the past six weeks. The work done by its two Company commanders is more than I thought possible. Since we came to France I think the rank and file have never been more severely tried.

The needs of the Army required the Battalion to hold a most important section of the line without being given time to reorganize after the losses of the 25th Sept. The 4th answered that call, and, in the spirit of the traditions of the Black Watch, performed the hard labour asked of it.

Army Form C. 2118.

1/4th Bn. The Black Watch T.F.

WAR DIARY
or
INTELLIGENCE SUMMARY.
(Erase heading not required.)

Place	Date	Hour	Summary of Events and Information	Remarks and references to Appendices
			Appendix 1 (contd).	
			It is with great regret that I leave the 4th Black Watch. I wish the Battalion was to come with the 2nd Battalion, and that we could continue fighting side by side as we have done for the past nine months.	
			But I am also glad that my representations will soon be carried out, and that a separate Commanding Officer will be appointed to the 4th, or who, though he cannot have at heart more than I have, will be able to devote his whole time to the needs of the Battalion.	
			I hope, too, that my several representations will be attended to, and that the Battalion will be given a long and well-deserved rest out of the trenches.	
			On behalf of the 2nd Battalion I wish the 1/4th all good fortune. I can wish the Battalion nothing better than they continue to fight in the same gallant way that	

T2131. Wt. W708—776. 500000. 4/15. Sir J. C. & S.

Army Form C. 2118.

1/4 & Bn. The Black Watch T.F.

WAR DIARY
or
INTELLIGENCE SUMMARY.
(Erase heading not required.)

Place	Date	Hour	Summary of Events and Information	Remarks and references to Appendices
			Appendix 1 (cont'd)	
			distinguished their attack on September 25th, and that they will	
			show to my successor the same fine spirit of discipline they	
			have shown to me.	
			(Signed) A.G. Wauchope, Lt-Col,	
			Commanding	
			2nd and 1/4th (T.F.) Battalions	
			The Black Watch	
In the Field,				
4-11-15.				

1/4th Bn The Black Watch, T.F.

Casualty List for the Month of November, 1915.

Date	Killed	Wounded	Missing	Sick	Accidentally Killed	Accidentally Wounded
Nov 3				4		
5		1		2		
6				1		
8				2		
9				2		
10				5		
11		3				
12				4		
13				3		
14				1		
15				4		
16				1		
19				1		3
22				1		
27		1				
29				2		
30				1		2
	—	5	—	34	—	5

Officer.
Nov. 5. Wounded — 2nd Lieut. P. M. Moon.

G M R Seales
Lieut-Colonel.
COMMANDING 1/4th BATT. THE BLACK WATCH (T.F.)

1/4th Bn. The Black Watch, T.F.

List of Officers joining as Reinforcements during the month of November, 1915.

Nov. 7	MAJOR	SCEALES, G.A.M.L.	from 1st A & S H.
" 12	LIEUT.	PLIMPTON, R.A.	from 13th A & S H.
" "	"	CURREY, R.F.	from 13th A & S H.
" "	2/Lt.	MITCHELL, A.	from 11th Gndn. H.
" "	"	JAMES, H.	from 11th Gndn. H.
" "	"	FINLAYSON, F.W.N.	from 11th Gndn. H.
" "	"	HOWARD BUCHANAN, F.H.	from 11th Gndn. H.
" "	"	MOSER, G.R.	from 13th A & S H.
" "	"	SCRATTON, G.H.	from 13th A & S H.
" 14	LIEUT.	ROBERTSON, W.S.	from 11th B.W.
" "	2/Lt.	MENZIES, J.D.S.	" 11th B.W.
" "	"	ANDREW, T.F.	" 11th B.W.
" "	"	OSBORNE, E.C.	" 11th B.W.
" 25	MAJOR	MUIR, J.B.	rejoined from Reserve Bn 4th B.W.

G.M.R. Sceales

Lieut-Colonel,
COMMANDING 1/4H BATT. THE BLACK WATCH (T.F.)

ATTACHED { 15TH DIVISION
44TH INFY BDE

39 DIVISION

118 BDE

1-4TH BN ROY. HDRS (BLK WATCH)

— - DEC 1915

Index

1/4th Black Watch

SUBJECT.

Lt Seafield

44/15

JF
6th?

No.	Contents.	Date.
	~~December~~ ~~September~~ 1915.	
	Came from Bareilly Bde 15.11.15 To 154th Bde 7.1.16.	

Army Form C. 2118.

WAR DIARY
or
INTELLIGENCE SUMMARY.
(Erase heading not required.)

Instructions regarding War Diaries and Intelligence Summaries are contained in F. S. Regs, Part II. and the Staff Manual respectively. Title pages will be prepared in manuscript.

Place	Date	Hour	Summary of Events and Information	Remarks and references to Appendices
			Confidential. War Diary of 1st/4th Battn. The Black Watch (R.H.) T.F. from 1st December 1915 to 31st December 1915 (Volume) IV XVth Divn Glenrinnes Lieut-Colonel, COMMANDING 1/4th BATT. THE BLACK WATCH (T.F.)	

Army Form C. 2118.

WAR DIARY
or
INTELLIGENCE SUMMARY.

(Erase heading not required.)

1/4th Bn. The Black Watch. T.F.

Place	Date	Hour	Summary of Events and Information	Remarks and references to Appendices
FRANCE				
	Dec 1		Battn. moves to French Line. B Coy. by bus to PHILOSOPHE. Two platoons thence to trenches and attached to 10th Gordons. A Coy and Detachments to LABOURSE and thence by bus to PHILOSOPHE. Entered by communication trenches from Notes on Trenches.— VERMELLES. Communication Trenches very good till the old British line is reached. Our portion of the trenches opposite the Quarries from the Hairpin and Goleen Alley	BETHUNE 2nd Edn. 1-40,000
	4		Two officers are attached to each of the other four Battns of the Brigade	
			Two platoons B Coy. when relieved, billeted in huts at NOYELLES.	
	10		Leave allotment of 14 places daily given to Battn.	
	14		Battn relieved from trenches and moves back to Divisional Rest.	

Army Form C. 2118.

WAR DIARY
or
INTELLIGENCE SUMMARY.
(Erase heading not required.)

1/4th Bn. The Black Watch T.F.

Place	Date	Hour	Summary of Events and Information	Remarks and references to Appendices
	Dec. 14 (cont.)		Transport goes by road, brigaded. Battn. marches to NOEUX-LES-MINES, thence by train to LILLERS, and thence by road to ALLOUAGNE. In billets there.	"FRANCE" BETHUNE 2nd Edn 1-40,000
			Leave allotment reduced to 6 daily	
	15		Large numbers of courses of instruction in Machine Gunnery, Trench Mortar Gunnery	
	15-16		Time devoted to cleaning of uniform, etc.	
	17		Commencement of Company training.	
	21		No. 8627 C.S.M. Scott, R., joins Battn. as R.S.M.	
	22		Major G.A.McL. Sceales authorised to assume rank of Temp. Lieut-Col.	

Army Form C. 2118.

WAR DIARY
or
INTELLIGENCE SUMMARY.
(Erase heading not required.)

1/4th Bn The Black Watch, T.F.

Place	Date	Hour	Summary of Events and Information	Remarks and references to Appendices
	1915			FRANCE
	Dec. 25.		Draft of 5 Sgts, 2 L/Sgts, 1 Cpl, 14 L/Cpls, and 126 men join Battn. Formation of new Company (D), consisting of one Platoon from A, one from B, and two from D Coys. Company commanders are now:-	SETTINGS 2nd Edn 1-4-3-500
			<u>A</u>: 2nd Lt. R.G. CUNNINGHAM. <u>B</u>: Lieut. T. STEVENSON.	
			<u>C</u>: Lieut. G.R. DONALD. <u>D</u>: Lieut. A. WATT.	
	29.		Rifle range in sandpit at disposal of Battn.	
	31.		During the month the gas helmet satchel has been taken into wear in the position of a sporran.	

1/4th Bn. The Black Watch, T.F.

Casualty List for the Month of December 1915.

Date	Killed	Wounded	Missing	Sick	Accidentally Killed	Wounded
Dec 1		1				
5	2	7		1		
6		1		2		
9				2		
10				2		
11						
14				1		
16				1		
26				2		
30				1		
31				1		
	2	9	—	13		

G.H.R. Peebles.

Lieut-Colonel,
COMMANDING 1/4H BATT. THE BLACK WATCH (T.F.)

ATTACHED { 51ST DIVISION
154TH INFY BDE

39DIV
118BDE

1-4TH BN BLACK WATCH
(ROY.HIGHLANDERS)
JAN-FEB 1916

Army Form C. 2118.

WAR DIARY
or
INTELLIGENCE SUMMARY.
(Erase heading not required.)

154 Bde / 51

From 154 Bde
6.1.16

LI Divⁿ

Confidential

War Diary
of
1st/4th Battⁿ The Black Watch (R.H.) T.F.

from 1st January 1916 to 31st January 1916

(Volume 4) V

Bill Neish.
Lieut-Colonel
COMMANDING 1/4th BATT. THE BLACK WATCH (T.F.)

Army Form C. 2118.

WAR DIARY
or
INTELLIGENCE SUMMARY.   4th Bn. The Black Watch (R.H.)

(Erase heading not required.)

Instructions regarding War Diaries and Intelligence Summaries are contained in F. S. Regs., Part II. and the Staff Manual respectively. Title pages will be prepared in manuscript.

Place	Date	Hour	Summary of Events and Information	Remarks and references to Appendices
ALLOUAGNE (Allouagne)	Jany 1-5		At ALLOUAGNE. Time devoted to training.	FRANCE BETHUNE 2nd Edition 1/40,000
	6		Battalion left ALLOUAGNE at 8 a.m., entrained at LILLERS at 9.51 a.m to LONGUEAU and marched to RAINNEVILLE, near AMIENS, arriving about 10 p.m. Joined 154th Infantry Brigade, 51st (Highland) Division, XIII Corps (R.R.Gp.1) (Pa. Mason) Third Army.	FRANCE AMIENS 17 1/100,000
	7-8		In Billets at RAINNEVILLE. Company training commenced.	
	9		2/Lieut. G.R. MOSER appointed Battalion Intelligence Officer.	
	10		Battalion Lewis Gun team formed under 2/Lieut. H. JAMES.	
	11		Inspection by Brig.-General C.E. STEWART, Comdg. 154th Infantry Brigade. Brig. General C.E. STEWART expressed himself as very pleased with the appearance and turn-out of the Battalion on parade. The commanding Officer considers that the improvement in this respect reflects highly on the efforts of all ranks from Company Commanders downwards.	
	12		Draft of 23 other ranks joined Battalion.	
	14		154th Brigade Machine Gun Company formed - Detachment of 2 Officers and 29 (other)	

Army Form C. 2118.

WAR DIARY
or
INTELLIGENCE SUMMARY.
(Erase heading not required.)

1/4 Bn. The Black Watch (R.H.) T.F.

Place	Date	Hour	Summary of Events and Information	Remarks and references to Appendices
	Jany 4		other ranks from this unit joins Brigade Machine Gun Company.	
			Officers:- 2Lieut. J. M^cMASTER and 2Lieut. F.W.N. FINLAYSON.	
	16		2Lieut. G.R. MOSER attached to Royal Flying Corps on probation.	
			Lieut. R.F. CURREY appointed Battalion Intelligence Officer vice 2/Lieut. G.R. MOSER.	
			2Lieut. R.C. CUNNINGHAM and No. 1683 C.S.M. MORRISON went to Third Army School of Instruction for a course of training.	
			The following are extracts from the "London Gazette":-	
			Mentioned in despatches (Jany 10th):-	
			Major J.S.Y. ROGERS	
			Capt. R.W. M^cINTYRE	
			Lieut. T. STEVENSON	
			R.S.M. W. CHARLES.	
			To be Companion of the Distinguished Service Order (Jany 4):- Major J.S.Y. ROGERS	
			The Military Cross:- Capt. R.W. M^cINTYRE.	
	19		Range placed at disposal of "D" Coy.	

Army Form C. 2118.

WAR DIARY
or
INTELLIGENCE SUMMARY. 1/4 Bn. The Black Watch (R.H.) T.F.
(Erase heading not required.)

Place	Date	Hour	Summary of Events and Information	Remarks and references to Appendices
	Jany 20		Corps Commander inspected transport at 2.15 p.m.	
	21		Battalion takes place in Brigade Field Day. Battalion under command of Major J.B. MUIR forms part of a Red Force commanded by Lieut-Col G.A. McL SCEALES. Lieut J.L. PULLAR acts as Staff Officer to the Red Force and Lieut. R.F. CURREY as Battalion Adjutant.	
	23		Lieut W.F. WILKIE and three N.C.O.'s proceed to Divisional Training School for a course of training.	
	24		The Army Commander approves the appointment of Lieut. J.L. PULLAR as Adjutant, vice Major F.R. TARLETON, with effect from 26th Septr. 1915.	
	24.		Battalion takes place in a Brigade Field Day. Battalion under command of Major J.B. MUIR forms part of a Red Force commanded by Lieut-Col. G.A. McL SCEALES. Lieut J.L. PULLAR acts as Staff Officer to the Red Force, and Lieut. R.F. CURREY as Battalion Adjutant.	
	25.		Battalion inspected by Major-General G.M. HARPER, C.B., D.S.O., Comdg 51st (Highland) Division.	
	31		Gas Demonstration by the Chemical Adviser, 3rd Corps.	
	29		Lieut J.L. PULLAR goes to Hospital, and 2/Lt G.H. SCRATTON becomes Acting Adjutant.	

T2134. Wt. W708-776. 500000. 4/15. Sir J.C. & S.

1/4th Bn. The Black Watch (R.H.). T.F

Casualty List for the month of January 1916.

	Sick.	
Jany 2.	1	
3.	3	
5.	1	
6.	3	
7.	1	
11	1	Detached - to Bde Machine Gun Coy.
14	2	29.
16	1	
17	15	
24	1	
25.	2	
26	6	
29	2	
	39	

Officers.

Jany 14. 2/Lieut J. McMASTER & 2/Lieut F.W.N. FINLAYSON detached to Bde. Machine Gun Coy.

Jany. 29. Lieut J.L. PULLAR Sick.

G.M.R. Scarlet
Lieut-Colonel,
COMMANDING 1/4th BATT. THE BLACK WATCH (T.F.)

1/4th Bn. The Black Watch (R.H.) T.F.
State for 1st January 1916.

	Officers	A	B	C	D	Total
A. Trench Strength.						
Duty	14	143	141	-	158	442
Machine Gunners	1			31		31
Stretcher Bearers				12		12
Signallers				18		18
First Aid Post				2		2
Sanitary Squad				7		7
Hd. Qrs.	4			16		16
Servants				2		2
At Courses of Instruction	3		3	5	3	11
Total	22	143	144	93	161	541
B. Non-Trench Strength.						
Officers Mess				1		1
Orderly Room				3		3
Transport				19		19
Grooms			1	3	1	5
Coy. Employ		3	3	1	1	8
Q.M's "	1			18		19
Leave	4		10	40	6	56
Absent without leave		4	2	3	5	14
Brigade Employ		2	2		3	7
Brigade Mortar Gun Coy	1			12		12
	28	152	162	193	148	685

G M Scales
Lieut-Colonel,
COMMANDING 1/4H BATT. THE BLACK WATCH (T.F.)

Army Form C. 2118.

WAR DIARY
or
INTELLIGENCE SUMMARY.
(Erase heading not required.)

Went 1/8 Bde (29 2) 27.2.16. Feb 27"
51 Divn [transferred to XXIX*]

Confidential.

War Diary
of
1st/4th Battn. The Black Watch (R.H.) T.F.

From 1st February 1916 to 29th February 1916.

(Volume 2) VI.

GM Sceh.
Lieut-Col
COMMANDING 1/4TH BATT. THE BLACK WATCH (T.F.)

Army Form C. 2118.

WAR DIARY
INTELLIGENCE SUMMARY. 1/4th Bn The Black Watch (R.H)

(Erase heading not required.)

Place	Date	Hour	Summary of Events and Information	Remarks and references to Appendices
RAINNEVILLE, Somme	February		During the month 14 Officers and 428 other ranks were inoculated against typhoid.	Map "RANGE" 1/39,000
	Feb. 1.		Gas demonstration given in a barn by the Chemical Advisory 3rd Army. After the contents of a gas cylinder had spread through the barn, all Officers, NCO.s and men on parade, wearing gas helmets of the tube pattern, were marched through.	
	2.		The Battn took part in a Brigade scale march as part of in continuation of an extensive training scheme	
	6.		The Battn moved to billets at CO.SY.	
			Reinforcements: 2/Lieut S.C. THOMSON, posted to B Coy, and 2/Lieut C.S. McCRIRICK, posted to D Coy, from 3/4th Black Watch.	
	7.		The Battn moved to billets at LA NEUVILLE.	
	9.		Reinforcement: Capt: E.A. SHEPHERD from 3/4th Black Watch. Capt: J.O. DUNCAN from 3/4th Black Watch.	
	12.		The Battalion took part in a Brigade Field Day being part of a Khaki Force commanded by Lieut-Col. BEATON, 4th Cameron Highlanders.	

Army Form C. 2118.

WAR DIARY
or
INTELLIGENCE SUMMARY.
(Erase heading not required.)

1/4th Black Watch (R.H.) T.F

Place	Date	Hour	Summary of Events and Information	Remarks and references to Appendices
	Feb.	13	Reinforcement: Capt: E.L. BOASE and 2/Lt: V. GLOVER from 3/4th Black Watch.	
		16	On receipt of orders Major Muir, in the absence of Lieut. Col. SCEALES, went, together with the Commanding Officer of the 5th Battalion Black Watch, to G.H.Q. They were interviewed by Sir NEVILLE MACREADY, the Adjutant-General, who told them that it had been decided either to split up these two Battalions and draft them to other units of the Black Watch or to amalgamate them into one Battalion. Major MUIR said that, although he was personally much against either of the two alternatives, in his opinion the men would prefer the amalgamation. The Adjutant-General promised that it should be placed on record that at the end of the War there two Battalions should go home as the 4th and 5th Black Watch, and not as one Battalion.	
		17	Reinforcement: 2/Lt: N. HARLEY, from 3/4th Black Watch.	
		20	Draft of 1 Corporal and 6 men joined from 3/4th Black Watch. All but one man were trained signallers.	

Army Form C. 2118.

WAR DIARY
or
INTELLIGENCE SUMMARY.
(Erase heading not required.)

1/4th Black Watch (R.H.), T.F.

Place	Date	Hour	Summary of Events and Information	Remarks and references to Appendices
	Feb. 24		Arrival of a draft from the 3/4th Black Watch, comprising Lieut. A.J. STEWART, 3 sergeants, 2 lance-sergeants, 2 corporals, 7 lance-corporals and 48 privates (Total: 1 Officer, 62 other ranks). On the eve of the departure of the 1/4th Black Watch and two other Battalions from the Brigade a special order was issued in which Brigadier-General C.E. STEWART, C.M.G., commanding the 137th Infantry Brigade, bade farewell to those troops.	See Appendix 1.
	25		The Battalion proceeded by march route and train to G.H.Q. area, where it was to form temporarily of G.H.Q. Troops, under the command of Brigadier-General L.A.M. STOPFORD, C.B. After an early morning march from LA NEUVILLE to LONGEAU, the Battalion entrained and left at 10.33 a.m. for ST. OMER, whence, on arrival at 7.50 p.m., it went by road to the billeting area at RENESCURE. Snow had been threatening and falling lightly for some days. It commenced to snow hard when on the road about one mile from LONGEAU Station. General C.E.	

Army Form C. 2118.

1/4th Black Watch (R.H.) T.F.

WAR DIARY
or
INTELLIGENCE SUMMARY.
(Erase heading not required.)

Place	Date	Hour	Summary of Events and Information	Remarks and references to Appendices
	Feb. 27		STEWART and Capt. the Hon. E.V. CAMPBELL (Brigade Major) came to see the Battalion off and expressed great regret at its departure. On arrival at ST. OMER it was still snowing hard, and the march from the station there to RENESCURE was made in a blizzard. Though only six miles, with the snow falling underfoot and the road totally obscured and indistinguishable from the ditches and surrounding fields, the march was made under the most trying conditions, and men fell frequently. Very inadequate arrangements having been made, it was about 3.30 a.m. before all ranks who were more or less settled in.	
	29		Brigadier-General W. BROMILOW with his Brigade Major (Major S.E. Norris, the Rifle Brigade) and Staff Captain (Capt. the Hon. H. BERESFORD, Seaforth Highlanders) arrived about 10 a.m., having come direct from England to command the 118th Brigade. Brigade order No 1 by Brigadier-General W. BROMILOW, commanding 118th Brigade, forms the new Brigade comprising	

Army Form C. 2118.

WAR DIARY
or
INTELLIGENCE SUMMARY.
(Erase heading not required.)

1/4th Black Watch (R.H.), T.F.

Place	Date	Hour	Summary of Events and Information	Remarks and references to Appendices
			1/4th Royal Highlanders.	
			1/5th Royal Highlanders.	
			1/6th Cheshire R.	
			1/1st Cambridge R.	
			1/1st Herts R.	
			Heavy rain having fallen during the night, the snow almost completely disappeared.	

Appendix No. 1.
War Diary of 1/4 Black Watch,
Feb. 1916.

COMMANDING 1/4th BATT. THE BLACK WATCH (T.F.)

SPECIAL ORDER
by
Brigadier General C.E.STEWART, C.M.G.,
Commanding 154th Infantry Bde.

Thursday, 24th Feby. 1916.

On the departure of the 1/4th, 1/5th Battalions THE BLACK WATCH, and 1/4th Battalion Q.O.CAMERON HIGHLANDERS, the Brigadier General Commanding desires to place on record his appreciation of the high standard attained by these three distinguished Battalions during the past seven weeks in which all ranks have worked so well in the 154th Infantry Brigade, as well as his full recognition that they, whether individually or collectively, may be depended on to help most effectively in our mutual objects, the maintenance of civilization against and the subjection of the common enemies of humanity, who have broken every law, human and divine, in their mad lust for power.

The Brigadier General thanks all ranks of these three Highland Battalions for their loyal and cordial co-operation with him in the all too short time they and he have been together and trusts it may be his good fortune to serve with them again.

C.E.STEWART,
Brigadier General,
Commanding,
154th Infantry Brigade.

Brigade H.Q.,
24-2-16.

1/4th Bn The Black Watch (R.H.) T.F.
State for 1st February 1916

A. Trench Strength.

	Officers	A	B	C	D	Total
Duty	14	140	132		140	412
Lewis Gun Team	1			26		26
Stretcher Bearers				15		15
Signallers				18		18
First Aid Post				1		1
Sanitary Squad				6		6
Hd. Qrs.	3			14		14
Servants				3		3
At Courses of Instruction	2		11	5	7	23
	20	140	143	88	147	518

B. Non-Trench Strength.

	Officers	A	B	C	D	Total
Officers' Mess				3		3
Orderly Room		1		2		3
Transport	1			25		25
Grooms			1	4	1	6
Coy Employ		3	3	3	3	12
Q.M's	1	1		15		16
Leave	3	4	5	11	6	26
Absent without leave		3			1	4
Brigade Employ		6		5	2	13
Mortar Gunners				11		11
Hospital	1			6	1	7
	26	158	152	143	161	644

G.M. Scales
Lieut-Colonel

1/4th Bn. The Black Watch (R.H.) T.F.

Casualty List for the Month of February 1916

		Sick	Accy. wounded
Feb.	1.	5	
	3	2	
	4	2	1
	5	1	
	6	2	
	8	3	
	9	2	
	10	1	
	15	1	
	16	1	
	17	2	
	19	1	
	21	2	
	25	9	
	27	1	
	28	1	
		36	1	Grand Total 37.

Officers

February 3. Lieut. G. R. DONALD, sick.

[Note – Lieut. J. L. PULLAR, shown in the Diary for January as sick, was transferred to the U.K. on Feb. 16th.]

G M P Steples
Lieut.-Col.
COMMANDING 1/4th BATT. THE BLACK WATCH (T.F.)

Army Form C. 2118.

WAR DIARY
or
INTELLIGENCE SUMMARY.
(Erase heading not required.)

Instructions regarding War Diaries and Intelligence Summaries are contained in F.S. Regs., Part II. and the Staff Manual respectively. Title pages will be prepared in manuscript.

Place	Date	Hour	Summary of Events and Information	Remarks and references to Appendices

T2134. Wt. W708-776. 500000. 4/15. Sir J. C. & S.

1/4th Bn. The Black Watch (R.H.) T.F.

Officer Reinforcements in February 1916

Feb 6. 2/Lt C.S. McCRIRICK from 3/4th Black Watch
   "   "   S.C. THOMSON   "   "   "
   9. Capt: J.O. DUNCAN   "   "   "
   "   "   E.A. SHEPHERD   "   "   "
  13.   "   E.L. BOASE   "   "   "
   " 2/Lt V. GLOVER   "   "   "
  18   "   N. HARLEY   "   "   "
  24 Lieut A.J. STEWART   "   "   "

                                G.M.R. Seeks
                                           Lieut:- Col
                        COMMANDING 1/4h BATT. THE BLACK WATCH (T.F.)

Army Form C. 2118.

WAR DIARY
or
INTELLIGENCE SUMMARY.
(Erase heading not required.)

February 1916

Place	Date	Hour	Summary of Events and Information	Remarks and references to Appendices
	1916		Brigadier General & G Stewart CMG demanded 154th Infantry Brigade.	

On the departure of the Lt. 15th Bn. The Black Watch and Lt. Col. A.O. Cameron Highlanders, the Brigadier General Cameron desires to place on record his appreciation of the high standard attained by these two old battalions during the past seven years that he had served with them. They were as well in the 154th July Brigade as well as to all arrangements that they had independently made as to all organisation against... the tenure of... the commanding officers... have... been every... action of... since they had been in all the... the Brigadier General had... battalion... and clearly... their... in all the... which he took... to whom he had... the law, help, hopeful and trust it may be... future to... me out the again...

Brig. Gen....

39 DIV
118 BDE

1/4 BLACK WATCH
1916 MARCH (1st to 15)

CONFIDENTIAL

WAR DIARY
INTELLIGENCE SUMMARY.
(Erase heading not required.)

Army Form C. 2118.

GHQ Vol. VII

War Diary of
1/4th Bn The Black Watch

War Diary for March 1916.
From 1-3-16 to 15-3-16.

(Volume immediately after volume for February 1916)

G.W. Steele Lieut-Col;
Comdg 1/4th Black Watch

1/4th Batt. the Black Watch

Army Form C. 2118.

March WAR DIARY 1916.

INTELLIGENCE SUMMARY.
(Erase heading not required.)

Place	Date	Hour	Summary of Events and Information	Remarks and references to Appendices
			Reference: Map. HAZEBROUCK SA. 1/100,000.	
RENESCURE	1-6		In billets at RENESCURE where the occurrence of snowstorms & E4a. water lying on the fields hampered training.	E4a.
LA BELLE HOTESSE	7		The Battalion moved by march route to billets at & near LA BELLE HOTESSE in the billeting area of the 39th Division (Major-General Bernardiston commanding) The 1/5th Black Watch was in billets close by, & arrangements in detail for the amalgamation of the two Battalions were put in hand. Orders were received from the Adjutant-General for the formation of a nucleus to be sent to the Base.	F4d
	13		Rolls, based on present strength, were prepared for submission to the Brigadier-General showing the proposed re-formation of the Battalion as follows:- 22 Officers (including the Medical Officer) and 544 Other Ranks to remain with the Battalion. 11 Officers and 156 Other Ranks to go to the Base Depot as a nucleus with Capt. BOASE. C.L. in command, 2/Lt. McCRIRICK. C.S. as Adjutant and 2/Lt. COX. W.D.M. as Quartermaster Officer.	App. 1.

1/4th Batn. The Black Watch.

March WAR DIARY 1916.

INTELLIGENCE SUMMARY.
(Erase heading not required.)

Army Form C. 2118.

Place	Date	Hour	Summary of Events and Information	Remarks and references to Appendices
	13th (contd)		The redistribution of Other Ranks was as follows:-	
			Coy. Strength. For the Base For the Coy. Batln.	
			"A" 179 24 155.	
			"B" 180 37 143	
			"C" 167 36 131	
			"D" 174 59 115	
			700 156 + 544 = 700.	
			Of the 11 Officers chosen to go to the Base Details, four were placed on detached duty, did not go to Base Depot (See Appendices N[o]s 2 & 3 for Rolls of Officers and their disposal). What was to be known for a time as the Composite Battalion (i.e. all ranks of the two Battalions who were to amalgamate) paraded to-day for the first time, under Lieut-Col. G.A. McI SCEALES.	Nos. 2 and 3
	14th		The Composite Battalion was inspected by the G.O.C. 39th Division (Major-General N.W Bernardiston)	

1/4th Batta. The Black Watch
March WAR DIARY, 1916

INTELLIGENCE SUMMARY.
(Erase heading not required.)

Army Form C. 2118.

Place	Date	Hour	Summary of Events and Information	Remarks and references to Appendices
	15th		Inspection of the Composite Battalion by the 51st Army Commander (General Sir Charles Monro, K.C.B.) The amalgamation as constituted by the Commanding Officers in consultation, was today approved. The strength of the 1/4th Black Watch immediately before amalgamation was as follows:- 33 Officers, 691 Other Ranks. Of these, 22 Officers and 545 Other Ranks joined the Composite Battalion. The rest were posted to the Base Details. [From this day forward a single War Diary will be kept for the Composite Battalion, but copies will be sent home for the records of both the 1/4th and 1/5th Battalions, the Black Watch.]	

Appendix 1 to War Diary for March, 1916

<u>Confidential</u>   Copy.
                                                                                                    118/C/1.

O.C. 1/4th Black Watch.

1. The following procedure will be carried out to form the amalgamated Battalion to war establishment.

2. A small nucleus of each Battn. with the Office Records &c. to be sent to the Base and retained there until such time as the Battalions can be reformed.

3. The Surplus Officers and men to be sent to ~~this~~ the Base to await disposal.

4. A complete list of Surplus Officers to be sent to this Office, a report being made as to any who have had experience on the Staff.

5. The latest Copy of A.F. E.624 does not contain any proviso as to drafting men to other units. Will you therefore ascertain and report the number of Warrant Officers, N.C.O.s and men of the 1/4th and 1/5th Royal Highlanders who are unwilling to serve under the latest form of Imperial Service agreement.

Extract from A.G., G.H.Q., letter A/10725 dated 2/3/16.

                                        S. E. Norris, Major,
                                          Brigade Major, 118th Infy. Bde.

                                        G.M. Sceales
                                          Lieut.-Col,
                                        Cmdg. 1/4th Black Watch.

War Diary for March, 1916.

Appendix 2

Roll of Officers of 1/4th. Black Watch posted to the Composite Battalion.

Lieut-Col.	Sceales, G.A.McL.	Commanding Officer.
Major.	Muir, J.B.	Second in Command.
Capt.	Stevenson, T.	Commanding "B" Coy.
"	Cunningham, R.C.	Commanding "A" Coy.
"	Watt, A.	
"	Donald, G.R.	Commanding "H" Coy.
Lieut.	Stewart, A.J.	Lewis Gun Officer
"	Robertson, W.S.	
"	Currey, R.F.	Intelligence Officer.
"	Plimpton, R.A.	
"	Wilkie, W.F.	
"	Duncan, W.B.	
2/Lieut.	Menzies, W.B.	Brigade Trench Mortar.
"	Scratton, G.H.	Bombing Officer.
"	Andrew, T.F.	
"	James, H.	
"	Osborne, E.C.	
"	Buchanan, F.H.H.	
"	Gibson, C.M.	
"	Berry, J.L.	118th. Brigade Staff.
Lieut.	McLachlan, D.	Quartermaster.
Major.	Rogers, J.S.Y., D.S.O.	R.A.M.C. Medical Officer.

G.McL.Sceales
Lieut:-Col,
Cmdg 1/4th Black Watch

1/4th. Battalion The Black Watch.

War Diary for March 1916.

Appendix...3....

Roll of Officers of 1/4th. Black Watch posted to 4th/5th. Black Watch Reinforcements.

Capt.	Boase, R.L.	Commanding Right Half
"	Duncan, J.O.	Commanding "AR" Coy.
"	Shepherd, E.A.	Commanding "BR" Coy.
Lieut.	Cox, W.A.M	
2/Lieut.	McCririck, C.S.	
"	Mitchell, A.	
"	Thomson, S.C.	Attached to 118 M G Coy.
"	Prain, J.C.	Attached to 118th. M.G. Coy.
"	Cunningham, T.F.	Attached to 118th. M.G. Coy. Transport Officer.
"	Glover, V.	~~Detached.~~ Attached to 118 M G Coy
"	Harley, H.	~~Detached.~~ posted to Command 3G⁰ Ordnance Salvage Coy.

GMSeeles
Lieut-Col.
Cmdg. 1/4th Black Watch

WD — Appendix 4   War Diary for March, 1916.

1/4th Bn. The Black Watch (R.H.), T.F.
State for March 1st, 1916.

	Officers	A	B	C	D	Total
A. Trench Strength.						
Duty	22	165	161	2	160	488
Lewis Gun Team	1			20		20
Stretcher Bearers				15		15
Signallers	1			28		28
First Aid Post				2		2
Sanitary Squad				4		4
Headquarters	4			13		13
Servants				5		5
At Course of Instruction			6		5	11
Total	28	165	167	89	165	586
B. Non-Trench Strength.						
Officers' Mess		2		2		4
Orderly Room		1		1		2
Transport	1			31		31
Grooms			1	4		5
Company employ		4	3	4	3	14
Q.M.'s "	1			18		18
Leave	1	4	3	6	3	16
Absent without leave		2	1		1	4
Brigade employ						
Mortar Gun	1			9		9
Hospital	1	2	3	5	6	16
Grand Total	33	180	178	169	178	705

Attached A.S.C.   4
         R.A.M.C. 3
              ―――
              7

G.W. Seales
Lieut.-Col.,
Cmdg. 1/4th Black Watch

1/4th Bn. The Black Watch (R.H.), T.F.
State for March 15th, 1916,
showing strength immediately before amalgamation
with 1/5th Black Watch.

	Offrs	A	B	C	D	
A. Trench Strength.						
Duty	24	162	163	3	164	492
Lewis Gun.	1			19		19
Stretcher Bearers.				14		14
Signallers.	1			28		28
First Aid.				2		2
Sanitary Squad.			1	5		6
Headquarters.	4	2		13		15
Servants.				5		5
At Course of Instruction		3	5		3	11
Total	30	168	168	89	167	592
B. Non-Trench Strength.						
Officers' Mess.				2		2
Orderly Room.		1		1		2
Transport.	1			32		32
Grooms.			1	4	1	6
Company employ		3	5	3	2	13
Q.M. employ	1			17		17
Leave			1			1
Absent without leave		2	1			3
Mortar Gun.	1			9		9
Brigade employ		3		2		5
Hospital.		1	3	3	1	8
Total	33	178	179	162	171	690

Attached:
A.S.C. 4
R.A.M.C. 3
        ———
        7

G.H.R. Steeles
Lieut.-Col.
Cmdg. 1/4th Black Watch

War Diary for March, 1916.   Appendix 6.

1/4th Bn. The Black Watch (R.H.), T.F.

Changes in Officer Personnel, March, 1916.

March 5.   2nd Lieut. G. R. Moser (Argyll and Sutherland Highlanders), attached 1/4th Black Watch, transferred to First Wing, No. 2 Squadron, Royal Flying Corps.

G.M. Sceales.
Lieut.-Col,
Cmdg. 1/4th Bn. The Black Watch

Appendix 7.

Battle Casualty Return
March, 1916.
NIL.

G.M. Sceales
Lieut.-Col,
Cmdg. 1/4th Bn. The Black Watch

www.ingramcontent.com/pod-product-compliance
Lightning Source LLC
Chambersburg PA
CBHW081242170426
43191CB00034B/2013